CADES
The Dream of the Smoky Mountains
COVE

by Rose Houk
Photography by Bill Lea

Phyllis,
Best Wishes!
Bill Lea
10/20/2007

GREAT SMOKY MOUNTAINS ASSOCIATION

©2007 Great Smoky Mountains Association
Edited by Kent Cave and Steve Kemp
Designed by Christina Watkins
Typography and Production by Amanda Summers
Photograph on page 22 ©Mary Ann Kressig
Color photograph on page 68 and all historic photographs
    courtesy National Park Service
All other color photography ©Bill Lea
Printed in Hong Kong

1 2 3 4 5 6 7 8 9

ISBN 978-0-937207-56-7

Great Smoky Mountains Association is a private, nonprofit
organization which supports the educational, scientific, and
historical programs of Great Smoky Mountains National Park.
Our publications are an educational service intended to
enhance the public's understanding and enjoyment of the
national park. If you would like to know more about our
publications, memberships, guided hikes and other projects,
please contact: Great Smoky Mountains Association,
115 Park Headquarters Road, Gatlinburg, TN 37738
(865) 436-7318.
www.SmokiesInformation.org

Contents

*To
Wilma Dykeman
who was
always at home
in the
Great Smoky
Mountains.*

"I had never seen anything quite so beautiful, Cades Cove is the dream of the Smoky Mountains."
—REV. ISAAC P. MARTIN, 1890

4

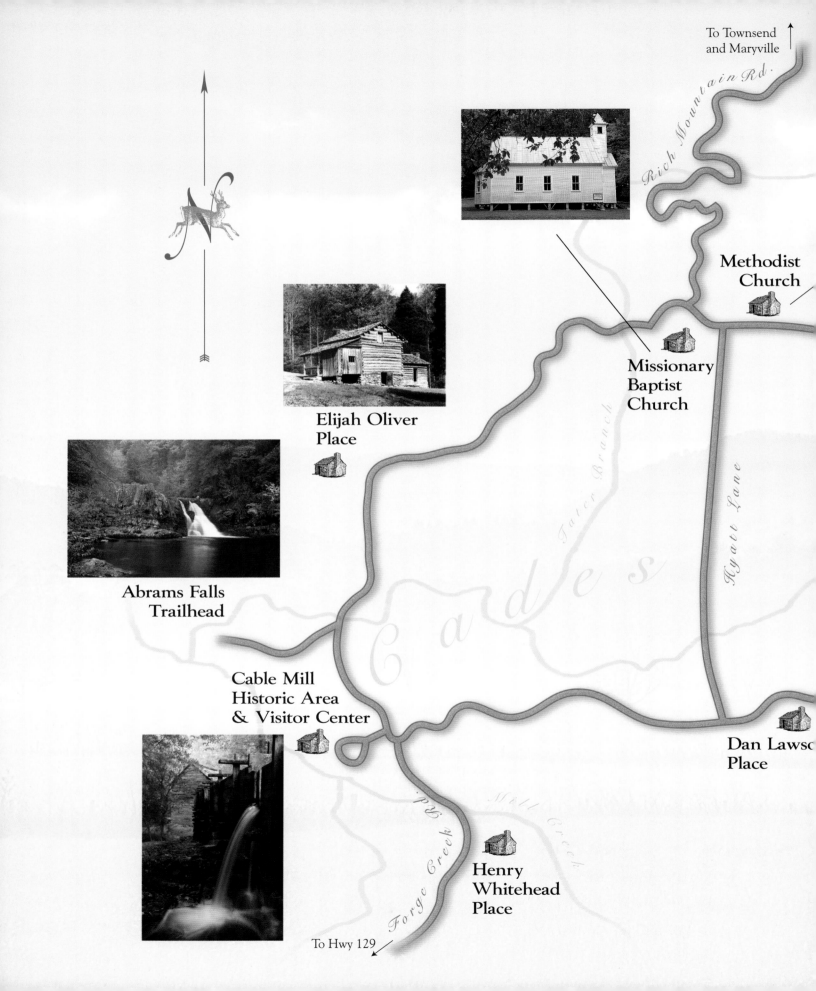

To Townsend
and Maryville

Rich Mountain Rd.

Methodist
Church

Missionary
Baptist
Church

Elijah Oliver
Place

Tater Branch

Hyatt Lane

Abrams Falls
Trailhead

Cades

Cable Mill
Historic Area
& Visitor Center

Dan Lawson
Place

Forge Creek

Mill Creek

Henry
Whitehead
Place

To Hwy 129

John Oliver
Place

imitive
ptist Church

Campground
Picnic Area

Start of one-way
Loop Road

Abrams Creek

Sparks Lane

Cove

Bades Cove Loop Road

Tipton
Place

Carter
Shields
Cabin

Every morning reveals a new Cades Cove to park visitors. Steeped in history, it is a dynamic place teeming with animal and plant life, where no two days are quite the same. That is why some "regulars" visit the cove over 100 times each year.

8

A Most Special Place

The gentleman at site B-1 in the Cades Cove Campground is obviously no stranger here. Bill Sharp seems to know just about everybody, and with good reason. He's been coming from his home in Knoxville to camp at Cades Cove for more than thirty years. He sets up his rig for a week at a time, always at the same site if he can get it. He hangs out a hand-routed wooden sign engraved with his name and that of his little dog, Miss Roxy.

On a rain-dampened October morning, the light dim and the air wet-cold, Miss Roxy curls up on her bed beside the fire. The embers glow orange within an ingenious campfire ring fashioned by her master from the innards of an old washing machine. Mr. Sharp sports a blue baseball cap, custom made just for him, embroidered in white with the words "Happiness is Cades Cove."

To neighboring campers he poses a question: what happened on Labor Day 1940? He waits patiently a moment, and met with blank stares he jumps in with the answer. That was the day President Franklin D. Roosevelt dedicated Great Smoky Mountains National Park at Newfound Gap. In his eighties now, Mr. Sharp has no trouble looking back through the years to see himself as an eighteen-year-old messenger boy for Western Union. His job on that momentous day was to pedal a bicycle from Newfound Gap to a telegrapher who was waiting to tap out the president's words to the nation and the world.

Bill Sharp has come with his family to the Smokies ever since, and Cades Cove is hands down his favorite place. He loves its "quietness" and believes he's probably driven the Cove

Loop Road "about a thousand times," often taking his grandson along to watch for deer. In the early days Bill and his wife came here in a Nash Rambler, folding down the car seats into a camper bed. He remembers when others arrived in big trucks covered with tarps—the people from the town of Alcoa, Tennessee, occupied one "street" in the campground, while those from Maryville took another.

To Mr. Sharp and many others, there's just something about Cades Cove that begs people to form a community.

Even the earliest visitors were taken with its beauty, people like Isaac P. Martin who approached the Cove on a fine sunny day in 1890. A circuit-riding Methodist minister, Martin was on his way to deliver the gospel to his extended congregation. Coming over Rich Mountain on the Tennessee side, Martin caught sight of the Cove through an opening in the trees. Topping out at a cliff, he gained a view down to the wide expanse entirely enclosed by high mountains. "I had never seen anything quite so beautiful," he exulted, "Cade's Cove is the dream of the Smoky Mountains."

The good reverend had touched on the essence of what makes the Cove so special. It's that bucolic scene of once-cultivated land set like a jewel amid a wilderness, the contrast of tidy meadow edging up to ragged forest. It's the dark silhouettes of deer emerging from thready morning mist. It's sturdy log cabins and barns tucked out of the wind, immaculate frame churches and well-tended cemeteries, water splashing over the big overshot wheel at the mill.

There's just something about Cades Cove . . . an irresistible combination of a human community and a natural one that stirs strong memories and brings people back again and again.

Even Franklin D. Roosevelt's triumphant dedication of the national park on September 2, 1940, was bittersweet for some. The transformation from home-place to public place meant that hundreds of families had to leave the Smokies. Today, millions come every year for sanctuary, adventure, and renewal.

For centuries the Cherokee hunted, fished, and harvested plants
in Cades Cove. So well did
they know the flora and fauna,
they had stories for many,
including otter, rabbit, bear,
rattlesnake, and deer.

Tsiyahi—"Place of the Otter"

A very long time ago, all the animals decided to hold an honor dance for the one with the most beautiful fur coat. They chose Otter, with his sleek dark pelt, and sent Rabbit to invite Otter to the dance. In truth, Rabbit envied Otter's gorgeous fur and so decided to play a trick. As they traveled back down the river to the village, Rabbit told Otter they should stop and camp for the night in a place where fire sometimes falls out of the sky.

Otter agreed, then Rabbit told him to take off his fur coat and hang it in a tree so it wouldn't get burned. Rabbit tossed campfire coals into the sky, frightening Otter so that he ran straight into the river for refuge. Then Rabbit grabbed Otter's coat and ran away. Back at the dance, Rabbit put on Otter's thick fur, and held his paw in front of his nose so no one would recognize him. But Bear wasn't fooled. He knew this was not his good friend Otter. Bear then revealed Rabbit's true identity to the others, and in anger snatched Rabbit's long tail.

The dancers went off to find Otter and return his coat, only to see that he was greatly enjoying the new idea of swimming in the river. Now all of Otter's descendants are found in the rivers and streams. And Rabbit sports only a little tuft of cotton for a tail.

To the Cherokee, who tell this cherished story, Otter is a familiar character. In fact, their name for Cades Cove was *Tsiyahi*, place of the otter, for the real river otters that swam in Abrams Creek. The English word "Cades" likely came from Cherokee Chief Kade, though others attribute it to Chief Abram's wife, Kate.

The *Aniyunwiya*, as the Cherokee call themselves, were living in Cades Cove when the first white settlers arrived in the early nineteenth century. The Cherokee had been in the Smoky Mountains since at least A.D. 1350, perhaps earlier. It was part of their immense homeland that included a large piece of the Southeast's geography—what are now the states of Tennessee and Kentucky, the Carolinas, and North Georgia.

But human presence in Cades Cove and vicinity extends much farther back in time. One tantalizing projectile point was found in the Tremont area not far from the Cove. Surmised to be about 10,000 years old, the sharp-tipped stone was likely made by a hunter who would have attached it to the end of a spear, which was then used to take down a bison or an elk. After the period of big-game hunters, over the next 2,000 years the climate and environment of the Appalachian Mountains changed drastically. As ice-age glaciers to the north receded, and spruce and fir trees retreated to the highest mountain-tops, the present

mix of hardwood forests came to enrich the southern Appalachians. People were adapting to these new conditions.

Some 6,000 to 4,000 years ago, native people first began to inhabit the Smokies in a substantial way. They kept moving with the seasons, taking advantage of everything the environment had to offer. They traveled up onto the grassy balds to hunt but also began to settle down for longer periods in the coves and valleys and on the floodplains. Hunters took deer with spears and with a "new" tool called an atlatl that made it possible to strike smaller creatures and from a greater distance. Plants assumed larger importance in their diet—especially the rich store of chestnuts that were gathered and ground on nutting stones. Soapstone vessels served as storage containers, and hearths and storage pits began to appear, clues to possible houses. (So far, though, no houses have been found in Cades Cove.)

The ensuing Woodland period, 3,000 to 1,000 years ago, was marked by a society that truly began to settle down in more permanent communities. Significant evidence points to this: structures built in villages on floodplains, pottery with a more elaborate check-stamped design, fabrics, burial mounds, and cultivation of corn, squash, and sunflowers.

The Woodland period, in the Smoky Mountains at least, leads straight into the Cherokee, with their oral history of Otter and many other animals. The Cherokee built winter round houses and summer rectangular homes of logs, with seven sides to correspond to their seven major clans. They first lived in dispersed settlements, then gathered in more sizable villages with council houses at the center. They relied more and more on the corn, beans, and squash they grew in fields they held in common.

A most prized plant was giant river cane that grew thick and tall along the streams and in moist woods. From it the Cherokee made spears, blowguns, and basketry. They scraped deer hides with bone tools and butchered meat with stone knives; they made soapstone pipes and effigy pots; and they dealt in trade beads and shell pendants. The Cherokee were well

connected in the region's economy, and several key trails met in Cades Cove.

Cherokee stories of Rabbit and Otter tell of a time when people were living in fine tune with the animals and plants, using what was available but also encouraging those things they wanted more of. The Cherokee cut the forests to make room for fields and to get firewood, and they burned certain areas regularly to nourish a bounty of nuts, berries, and deer.

In Cades Cove, Gregory Cave and a shallow pond called Lake in the Woods yield evidence of this environmental manipulation, along with clues to past climate. Preserved in Gregory Cave are plant pollen, cane torch marks on the cave roof, Woodland-period pottery, and the symbol of a turkey. The lake, north of the Cable Cemetery, revealed changes in plant life over the past 6,600 years. Forests went from oak, willow, and sweetgum, to more prolific growth of pines and cocklebur, suggesting disturbance of the land.

Nothing, it seems, remains the same. Despite a long history, the Cherokee community in Cades Cove would soon be replaced by another.

Relatively speaking, American Indians lived lightly on the land and left few observable reminders. Still, artifacts have been found in and around Cades Cove and a legacy of arts and crafts continues vibrantly to this day.

14

A Place Called Cades Cove

The arrival of Europeans in the southern Appalachians in the mid 1500s forever changed the lives of the Cherokee. In 1540, famed Spanish explorer Hernando de Soto was the first to come close to the Smokies. A little later, in 1557, a Spanish missionary found the Cherokee "dwelling in peace in their native mountains; they cultivated their fields and lived in prosperity and plenty."

But that prosperity was shattered in a devastating smallpox epidemic around 1728. The native people lacked immunity to this foreign disease, and as much as half the population perished. After the epidemic the Cherokee began concentrating in larger villages, one of which is known in Cades Cove. The site remains unexcavated, so archeologists are aware only of its barest outlines.

Still, the native people traded furs for the newcomers' horses and guns, fought alongside the British in the Revolutionary War, and generally tried to assimilate into the new culture. The Cherokee had a written constitution in their own language, from the syllabary devised by a man named Sequoyah. In the absence of public schools, they learned the words by teaching one another in cabins and along the roads.

Such strides meant little to those desiring Cherokee lands. The tribe ceded more and more territory in treaties with the United States government, including large sections in the Great Smoky Mountains. Even before it was legal, a land grant was issued in 1794 to one Hugh Dunlap for 5,000 acres "in a place called Cades Cove." In a couple more decades, Americans did enter the Cove, following the old Indian trails over Rich Mountain to the north and through Ekaneetlee Gap from the south.

Just as Sequoyah's syllabary was spreading among the Cherokee "like fire among the leaves," the first documented white settlers arrived in Cades Cove. The Olivers—John and Lucretia (also known as Lurena, Luraney, or Lucreta)—came from northeast Tennessee. They walked over the Rich Mountain Road in 1818 holding their new baby girl in their arms, heading for what they'd been told was good, unclaimed land in the Great Smoky Mountains. Legally, though, that part of the Smokies would not be ceded until a year later by the Calhoun treaty with the Cherokee. Even so, the local Indians brought food to the Olivers to help them survive what turned out to be a cold, snowy winter. The Olivers stayed to become the first permanent white settlers of Cades Cove.

In only a few years the trickle of pioneers swelled into a flood, and Cherokee hospitality was strained. With discovery of gold on Cherokee land in Georgia, that state simply confiscated the land. The federal government

Snow and cold are no strangers to the Great Smoky Mountains. Without the help of some Cherokee Indians, the first white settlers in Cades Cove may not have survived their initial winter.

then negotiated in bad faith, and finally in 1838 ordered the Indians rounded up. They were held for three months, then moved by boat and wagon, on ponies, or on their own feet to Indian Territory in Oklahoma. The Trail of Tears, as the year-long exodus is known, ended with several thousand Cherokee dead or displaced. Those who managed to hide out in the recesses of their Smoky Mountain homeland joined ranks with other Cherokee who already held title to reservation land to become the Eastern Band of Cherokee.

The Olivers soon had neighbors in Cades Cove, among them the Tiptons, Jobes, Cables, Shields, and Burchfields. Everyone's first order of business was to start a farm. The Cove bottomlands were saved for fields and pasture, while homes were built around the terraced edges. Farms generally were small, from ten to fifty acres, and property boundaries were recorded in deeds as leading from a corner "to the fifth row of corn," down to a stream "where an old sow swam the river," or at a tree marked "with a number of chops with a tomahawk on the north and west sides."

Much of the soil in the Cove was deep, fertile loam. A farmer hitched up a mule and plowed that rich ground, then planted rows of corn, wheat, oats, and rye. A flock of laying hens, a few beegums, and fruit trees were added soon enough. Still, not all Cove farmers enjoyed the best soil. Those with drier, sandier land would just get by, the ground worn out after a few years of cultivation. While the Olivers built in the higher, drier northeast end of the Cove, others such as Peter Cable ventured into the swampy, lower southwest end. He engineered dikes and drains to render the wet areas more habitable. On occasion, farmers were faced with floods on Abrams Creek. In 1886, it rained so many days that the creek waters rose and were reported "sweeping fences away, washing soil off and damaging meadows, wheat and oats on the bottomlands."

The National Park Service preserves the open nature of Cades Cove to reflect its mid-nineteenth century appearance when it was a successful farm community.

Mountain farmsteads were more than a house and barn. They might include a spring-house, meat house, apple house, corncrib, gear shed, tub mill, and blacksmith shop, each structure serving its own specific purpose.

Along with grain crops, nearly every family planted a vegetable garden. "We always had a garden," recalled Bonnie Myers whose North Carolina grandparents were among early Cove settlers. They saved their Irish seed potatoes, and along with them planted beans, cabbages, turnips, tomatoes, and a cornucopia of other produce. What they didn't eat fresh got dried, pickled, or cured.

Growing wild for the picking were all kinds of berries and an onion-like green called ramps. Like the Cherokee before them, the white settlers used fire selectively to nudge the land to better yields. "Used to the mountains would burn and that's what brought on the good berries," Bonnie remembered. "We'd pick those blackberries, and mama'd make jam and jelly, cooked with sugar cup for cup." Berry picking was a much-anticipated activity, and to help with the process a person carried an ingenious "hucklebucket" made of strips of tulip poplar bark formed into a container with a strap handle. Chestnuts were another highly valued food, before a blight wiped them out in the 1930s. In early September into October, said Cove resident Randolph Shields, "the nuts were gathered as they fell from the trees. It was no chore for a family to fill several bushel bags in a day."

Family and neighbors came together to share the work (and pleasures) of such chores as corn shucking, molasses making, apple peeling, and hog butchering.

Hubert Sullivan, who worked for twenty years as the miller at the Cable Mill, said "of a night in the winter we had a popper of corn" with popcorn they grew themselves. Hubert also told about cotton raised in the Cove—one of his

21

22

Farmers in the Cove summered their livestock on the alpine meadows they called "balds." Herders lived on the balds, tending the livestock for a per head fee. Today, some of the grassy balds remain and are home to colorful plants like flame azalea.

but the second John Oliver home, probably a distinct improvement over their first. It's a classic one-and-a-half-story log dwelling—the spaces between the logs are chinked with mud, a stout fieldstone chimney rises on one side, and the roof is covered with wood-shake shingles. A snake fence zigzags around the house, that would have enclosed a dirt yard kept neatly swept. The yard was the place where clothes were washed, hogs were scalded, and the garden was grown. Beyond the yard stood the all-important outbuildings—barn, springhouse, corncrib, pig pen, and others where tools and equipment and livestock and feed stayed dry under a roof. Perishables like butter and milk cooled on the damp rocks in the shaded springhouse, and country hams cured in the smokehouse.

jobs when he got home from school was to pick it for use in warm, colorful patchwork quilts.

As did most mountaineers, people in Cades Cove also hunted and trapped deer, bear, squirrels, rabbits, minks, and muskrats and fished for brook trout. In the early years they used percussion cap rifles, cane poles, and "fall" traps. Hubert Sullivan went "still hunting" in the fall without dogs, when the leaves were still on the trees and squirrels were up in them "working on hickory nuts." Other times, he hunted raccoons at night with his dogs.

While Cove residents worked without cease to feed themselves, they also had to put a roof over their heads. Settlers cut logs from towering tuliptrees, pines, or oaks; carefully notched the corner ends; and laid up the logs to make a small cabin, often with loft and front porch. John and Lucretia Oliver's cabin at the northeast end of the Cove was among the first. What visitors see today is not their original, however,

Most Cove families kept a few beef cattle, along with a milk cow, chickens, pigs, and sheep. In summer they grazed their stock up on Gregory and Parson balds and Spence and Russell fields. (In fact, Gregory Bald was then so treeless that from one side the broad expanse of Cades Cove was in full view far below.) These high-elevation meadows proffered green grass, cooler temperatures, and fewer insects. The drives up to the balds would have been a sight, and a sound, to behold with cowbells clanging and dogs barking alongside. Several families combined herds—cattle, sheep, hogs, a few horses and mules too—and various ownership was told by a distinctive earmark or a brass ring on an animal.

The stock drives got bigger and bigger as the years went on—herds from surrounding counties joined until more than a thousand animals were involved. Usually they headed up to the pastures in early May, risking a late snow-storm that could kill cattle.

Up on the balds, a herder tended the animals. He put out salt licks, rounded up the cattle in a storm, and warded off the occasional bear or wild cat. A main qualification for the job was the ability to call the cattle with a loud, drawn-out "sue-cow" or something equally persuasive. For his work, a herder charged a dollar or two per head. Around Labor Day, the cattle were corralled in a "gant lot" for two or three days to become gaunt from not eating. The belief was that the animals would fare better on the trip back to the lowlands if they weren't bloated by feeding on too much grass. They were taken back down at that time of year to avoid grazing a plant that caused "milk sickness."

The herders were legends in their own time. Among them were men like Russell Gregory, Dan Myers,

24

Fonz Cable, and Tom Sparks, who oversaw the Spence Field range. Sparks was a Cades Cove resident, so he spent weekends back down at his home. One Sunday night Tom was headed back up to the bald. He was a little late getting there and got tangled in a laurel thicket where he heard a "fuss." To his surprise, he finally located the source of the sound—a woman and her small baby lost in the dark. Tom told her to grab his shirt tail and he took her to his cabin. In the morning, he showed her back to "the top of Smoky Mountain" where she could find the road home.

Memories are keen about the murder of Tom Sparks. It was 1926. He was shot in the back by a young man in an altercation reportedly involving moonshine and those who made it.

Moonshine made from corn mash was a cash crop for some in Cades Cove. Corn was also fed to the animals, but mostly it was consumed by people, and most of that took the form of cornmeal for bread. Some families had their own small tub mills to grind meal for personal use. Eventually, though, the Cove held seven or eight larger overshot gristmills, including John Cable's mill.

A child's job on Friday nights was shelling corn, which then went to the mill on Saturday by horseback or wagon. If customers arrived outside regular hours, they rang the bell and waited for John Cable to come out of his field and start the

Cades Cove churches were filled with passion, but few adornments. There was singing, praying, and repenting but not much in the way of stained glass or ornate altars.

mill. Every miller took out an eighth of the corn in payment (about a gallon out of a bushel), which he could later use in trade.

When he came to work in the morning, the miller occasionally surprised a snake, a bear, or a bobcat rummaging down in the lower level of the mill. All day the miller sat in a dimly lit corner, watching the watergate and listening closely to the continuous lulling *whoosh-whoosh* of the wheel, indicating the turning speed was just right. Too fast and the meal would burn.

John Cable built his gristmill in the west end of the Cove around 1870. Standing for close to 140 years, it still operates today, powered by the same source of water splashing down the flume from Mill and Forge creeks. The water spills over white oak "buckets" on the giant wheel outside the two-story frame building. As the wheel turns, it powers gears inside, attached to a wooden spindle called the "damsel" that extends down through the center of a pair of round granite stones. The top, or running, stone moves against the lower, stationary bedstone. Corn is chuted between the stones, whose grooved surfaces reduce it to a fine meal that spills out warm and soft as talc. Cable's was a custom mill, grinding meal fine or coarse depending on a customer's preference. In one hour it could produce 150 pounds of meal.

At one time Cable Mill had a water-powered sash saw that cut boards for houses and barns. With that material available, after 1900 many Cove folks started building frame structures or covering their log homes with weatherboarding. Another product in high demand was iron—for a kettle, a bell, a hoe, or set of horse shoes. Fortunately there was iron ore in Cades Cove, and a large forge was built just

upstream from the Cable Mill. It was built in 1827 by Daniel D. Foute, entrepreneur and big landowner in the Cove in those days. Ore came from a mile away, and charcoal to fire the forge furnace was made from forest timber. Foute's "bloomery" forge was so called because the chunks of iron that were produced were called "blooms." Many an old timer remembered the sound of the 500-pound hammer reverberating through the acoustic bowl of the Cove, a sound heard until the forge closed about 1847.

On Sundays, it was an unspoken rule that people ceased work and observed the Sabbath. Religion took hold early in the Cove, and at first people met and prayed in each other's homes. Under the lead of John and Lucretia Oliver, a Baptist Church was started around 1825. John Oliver's son, Elijah, served the important role of church clerk for many years; Elijah's son, William, was the minister for nearly sixty years.

A difference of opinion developed among the Cades Cove Baptists around 1840, which led to a split between those who adhered to what they perceived as a more literal interpretation of scripture and those who believed in reaching out with missionaries. The original group called themselves the Primitive Baptists, while the others became Missionary Baptists.

In 1887, the Primitive Baptists replaced their old log church building with a new one. It still stands just off the loop road (not far from the Missionary Baptist Church), and visitors can step inside when the doors are open, perhaps attend a Sunday service, and stroll the grounds of the cemetery out back where John and Lucretia Oliver, Russell Gregory, and other early Cove settlers were laid to rest. This church featured "modern" improvements—a woodstove, "window lights" plus kerosene lanterns, and a ceiling of pine boards. Beyond that, it was spare and unadorned. Men sat on one side in the straight-backed wood pews, women on the other. At age twelve, when a child was baptized, he or she moved from the mother's side to the father's. When the church bell rang, people filed in dressed in their Sunday best. The service was participatory. If someone lost a family member,

they'd simply come to the front and pour out their grief in song. If another wanted, he'd walk up and join in too. The "elder," rather than a pastor, preached the sermon. The congregation joined in with the familiar hymns, "Amazing Grace," "I'll Fly Away," and "In the Sweet By and By." They read the music by the shape of the notes, and the strains flowed out the church doors and filled the surrounding woods. There were Methodists in the Cove too, and minister J. D. McCampbell constructed their church building in 1902—it took him 115 days and he charged a dollar a day.

Whatever the denomination, religion in Cades Cove was firmly anchored by a fundamental, and rock-solid, faith. It involved emotional revivals, footwashings, and funerals. People nurtured a firm belief in the hereafter—the body would soon enough join the loved ones in the cemetery, while the soul would rise up to that better home in the sky.

When a person died, the church bell chimed the number of years he or she had lived. People usually knew by the number of rings who had passed. Out of respect, they left the fields and attended to a solemn ritual. While the women prepared the body and readied the wake, the men, said coffin maker John McCaulley, would "just walk right out [of their own fields], go home, go to the graveyard, help dig the grave, go to helpin' make the casket. They'd help carry that funeral in there—nobody worked until that funeral was over with." Relatives and friends have upheld the long-standing tradition of laying flowers on the graves on Decoration Day, at the end of May or early June.

For many, the ever popular image of the Methodist Church nestled in the rich autumnal forest represents sanctuary and a spiritual relationship to nature.

Most of the important social events in Cades Cove had to do with church. There were singing schools, Sunday schools, baptisms, Decoration Days, foot-washings, and of course, dinners on the grounds.

The church in Cades Cove, especially the Primitive Baptist, exerted so much control over the community's residents it has been called an "invisible government." Those who didn't conform or who behaved improperly were well known and ostracized. Most notable were the citizens of Chestnut Flats, a small but notorious group in the southwest corner of the Cove who were given to general debauchery and lawless behavior. The "Flats"—renowned for moonshining, prostitution, card playing, and its share of murders—deeply offended the sober, upright residents of the Cove. George Washington Powell—Civil War veteran, justice of the peace, and merchant—was a pillar of the "Flats." From the fruit of some 2,000 apple and peach trees in his beautiful orchard, he distilled "fine brandies," sometimes legally, sometimes not. Powell also made moonshine, leading John Oliver to brand him and others of his kind as nothing better than "public outlaws."

In 1878 the state of Tennessee declared whiskey-making illegal. But moonshining was so profitable that Powell couldn't see giving it up. In September of 1878, a special deputy and eight men raided his "rum-mill" and found a fair amount of incriminating evidence. According to the *Maryville Index*, "eleven tubs of beer and mash, four tubs of pomace,

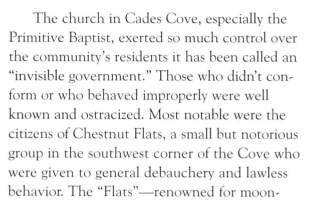

Baptism was a central rite of passage, especially for the Baptist congregations. The waters of Abrams Creek served this sacred purpose often and well.

one hundred and thirty gallons of brandy singlings, five bushels of meal, two bushels of rye and two bushels of malt" were seized and destroyed. When the agents tried to arrest Powell, he fled. As the enforcers headed back to town, they were ambushed and "a lively fusilade ensued." Forty-some shots were fired, the revenuers returned the fire, but no one was hurt. The report did not reveal the whereabouts of the fugitive.

The civilizing force of education came early to the Flats and the rest of the Cove. Families recognized the value of schooling for their children, so much so that they pooled their own money to pay a visiting teacher for a few months of the year. Abraham Jobe remembered the "old field schools" where "It was study from morning till noon, then an hour for playtime, and study from 1 o'clock till turning out time." Jobe felt he received a good education, and he ended up becoming a physician. By the mid 1800s, the Flint School was the first formal place of instruction in the Cove.

The Laurel Springs and Cable schools followed. In 1915 the two-story "consolidated" school was built in the center of the Cove, complete with library, auditorium, and basketball court. At school, students learned to debate, recite, and spell—spelling bees fomented heated competition between students. The Blue Back Speller and the Bible were required reading for everyone. To get a higher education, however, a young person had to leave the Cove.

"Aunt" Becky Cable

ebecca Cable was one of the most exceptional—and most loved— residents of Cades Cove. She was born in 1844, one of nine children of John P. and Elizabeth Cable. "Aunt" Becky never married and was tough as her own iron pitchfork. She ran her own farm in a hollow up off Mill Creek known as Becky's Sugar Cove and worked in her fields like any man—often without shoes on. Becky would shed her shoes, sling them over her arm, and tramp about barefoot all day. One time she stepped on a rattlesnake but fortunately the benevolent creature didn't strike.

She was a fine cook, and her apple pie made with "biscuit dough" and sweetened fruit was a coveted recipe. Becky put up boarders in her home, helped her brother tend their jointly owned general store, and took care of his children after he died.

Becky also raised sheep; carded, spun, and dyed the wool; and wove and knitted beautiful coverlets and clothing. One time she gave her friend John McCaulley a pair of wool socks in payment for all the coffins he'd made for Cades Cove families. McCaulley told Knoxville newspaperman Vic Weals that when he heard Becky had taken sick, he got the best yellow-poplar boards he could find and custom-made her coffin complete with six brass carrying handles. Becky got well that time, but when she did pass away, on December 19, 1940, at age ninety-six, her coffin was waiting for her.

Rebecca Cable was laid to rest "beneath a blanket of flowers" in the Cable Cemetery, not far from her big white farm house that was moved to the Cable Mill area after her death.

31

Some people pronounced Cades Cove as "Caged" Cove, they said because the mountains hemmed them in on all sides. That may have been how John Oliver and his neighbors felt, when they tried to take their corn, cattle, apples, butter, and eggs to outside markets. Eight men held ropes to wrangle the first wagon across Cades Cove Mountain. That was hard work, so it wasn't long before they started to improve the old Indian trails into passable roads. In 1838, Cove resident Russell Gregory oversaw construction of the Parson Branch Road, near Cable Mill, to connect with the Parsons Turnpike in North Carolina. But routes to the Tennessee towns of Maryville and Knoxville were even more desirable. The Joe Cooper Road was the first route out to Maryville, followed by another primary road, the old Indian Grave Gap trail over Rich Mountain to Tuckaleechee Cove. It was used for many years but was later relocated to the present Rich Mountain Road. John W. Oliver, the original John Oliver's great-grandson, said that "wagons of apples, cabbages, or logs went out, and white flour, 'a race of ginger,' baby's shoes, quinine, or dollars came back" along these rugged roads.

John W. Oliver, fresh from college in Louisville, Kentucky, returned home to the Cove with some newfangled ideas. One of his more radical notions was storing corn in a silo by his barn. He also introduced new animal breeds—Black Angus cattle, Berkshire boars, Brown leghorn hens, Italian bees—and instigated stocking of rainbow trout in Abrams Creek. A few neighbors ridiculed the idea, saying the fish would "all go over Abrams Falls and be deader'n four o'clock."

On June 28, 1833, Cades Cove got its first post office. At first, mail was delivered once a week from Sevierville. Everyone eagerly awaited the sound of the carrier's bugle from the top of Cades Cove Mountain, signaling he was on his way in. After the Civil War, mail delivery increased to three times a week and in 1904 to six days. In that year the Cove's renaissance man, John W. Oliver, won the job of mail carrier. He held the position for thirty-two years, riding horseback twenty miles a day. Also the preacher, Oliver was known to hang his leather mailbag on the pulpit at the Primitive Baptist Church to conduct a funeral service.

Communication with the world beyond the Cove was aided by installation of a battery telephone system in the 1890s. Dan Lawson did his part when he and his neighbors organized to build the line—strung from tree to tree—to Maryville. Residents learned what was going on in their midst when they gathered

Though surrounded by mountains, Cades Cove had at least five roads leading in and out. Parson Branch Road (following an old Indian trail) led to North Carolina, while Cooper Road led toward Maryville on the Tennessee side.

OVERLEAF—The mountains to the south and east are over a mile high and include rugged peaks such as Thunderhead and now legendary Rocky Top.

at Albert Hill's or Russell Burchfield's stores to swap news and trade their corn, chickens, or eggs for coffee, candy, cloth, coal oil, or other goods they couldn't provide themselves. In the 1930s, rolling stores—literally stores on wheels—came in regularly and offered some commercial competition.

If a baby was on the way, midwife Polly Harmon put her basket over her arm and set out to deliver a new citizen to the Cove. If a person took sick, he'd most likely consult a well-used copy of *Gunn's Domestic Medicine* guide for the proper herbal tea or a poultice, or self-medicate with camphor or liniment. If it was something really serious, he might go see old Doc Morton or Doc Saults.

Physicians like Dr. Thomas McGill were on hand to treat the more serious ailments that families couldn't take care of themselves. During most of the history of the community, one physician or another lived in the Cove.

Enormous change swept over the Great Smoky Mountains in the early twentieth century, with the advent of large-scale, industrial logging. An estimated two billion board feet of timber were removed from the Smokies' forests, affecting nearly 80 percent of what is now park land. Near Cades Cove was the logging boom town of Tremont, and not far away was a big mill in Townsend, named for Colonel W. B. Townsend, president of the Little River Lumber Company.

The potential for this type of logging in the Cove was there. In June 1904 *The Maryville Record* printed that "A report is current that the Little River Lumber Co. is about to extend its line over the ridge into Cades Cove to provide an outlet for alot of logs and lumber on the other side of the ridge." But long-held hopes for a logging railroad into the Cove never materialized, sparing the land some of the worst ravages inflicted by cutting the great trees. People were buying up select timber parcels in the Cove too, the biggest among them being Chicago lumberman Morton Butler who assembled more than 25,000 acres, with plans to cut the trees and run a large sawmill in the Cove. Creation of Great Smoky Mountains National Park put a halt to that idea.

Cove men did find work in the lumber camps—often walking many miles to a job, staying all week, then walking back home on the weekend with money in their pockets. The women and children stayed behind and tended the farm. Thus wage work and a cash economy grew at the expense of self-sufficient farming and a system of mutual barter.

Word spread early about the Cove's green fields and forests and its resourceful residents. In the 1880s author Mary Noailles Murfree,

The Civil War in the Cove

*I*t was brother against brother and neighbor against neighbor in the great national conflict of the nineteenth century. During the Civil War, most Cades Cove residents followed in the footsteps of east Tennessee and remained loyal to the Union. Some, though, sympathized with the Confederacy, among them Daniel D. Foute, one of the largest landowners in the Cove.

Western North Carolina, primarily Confederate, was literally just over the mountains from Cades Cove. This geographic proximity meant Rebel guerillas could more easily stage surprise attacks. And they did so, almost constantly. If Cove families had warning of their approach, they hid livestock, guns, farm goods, even themselves deep in the mountains. But if attacked without warning by the "bushwackers," help was hard to come by. For individual Cove farmers, writes historian Durwood Dunn, "the war experience was an intensely personal ordeal." Parents watched their sons go off to fight, and those who stayed behind often knew hunger and fear. Elders formed home guards and stood their ground. Russell Gregory was a member, and it cost him his life when guerillas entered his home one night in 1864 and killed him. Cades Cove reportedly was known as a station on the "underground railway" perhaps not for escaped slaves, but for Union soldiers who had fled Southern prisons and were headed north.

Institutions suffered too. The Primitive Baptists did not hold services for three years, from 1862 to 1865, "on account of the rebelion [sic] and we was union people and the Rebels was too strong here in Cades Cove." Although the war years were hard enough in the Cove, the after effects were bad, too. A general economic decline followed—demand for farm products dwindled, farm size was smaller, and land values dropped to five dollars an acre.

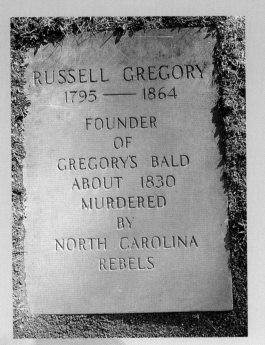

RUSSELL GREGORY
1795 — 1864

FOUNDER
OF
GREGORY'S BALD
ABOUT 1830
MURDERED
BY
NORTH CAROLINA
REBELS

By the early twentieth century Cades Cove was growing and becoming more easily accessible. Suddenly there were automobiles racing up and down the mud or gravel roads. Over 700 people lived in the Cove at this time, and for better or worse everybody seemed to know everybody.

writing under the pseudonym Charles Craddock, set several of her fictional, romantic stories in the Cove. Another, Robert Lindsay Mason, penned *The Lure of the Great Smokies* in 1927. By that time, a good new road was completed to Townsend, Tennessee. The first car, a Cadillac, had already arrived with A. J. Fisher of Walland behind the wheel in 1915. John W. Oliver opened a lodge to "good clean moral people, drunks and immoral people strictly prohibited," and a handful of intrepid hikers followed his lead along the trails to the balds. Other visitors toured the depths of Gregory Cave, paying fifty cents to follow a path lit by electric lights.

From the handful of pioneer families who first settled Cades Cove in the 1820s, the population grew, peaking at 685 people around the year 1850. Numbers dropped in the 1860s, after the depredations of the Civil War, but the 1900 census listed another population high—709 souls. By that time, the Cades Cove community was inhabited by several long-standing families, the Olivers, Burchfields, Cables, Myers, and others with strong ties to one another and to their Cove homes.

They held close knowledge of every rock, tree, spring, creek, and hill. The names they put on the map speak volumes—More Licker and Tater Branch, Mollies Ridge and Coon Butt, Panther Gap and Doe Knob. And while they knew their home ground intimately, they weren't as isolated and backwoodsy as stereotypes popularized by local colorists often suggested. Through newspapers, schools, relatives, and markets in larger towns, Cove residents maintained many outside connections.

Cades Cove developed into a close-knit community. Everyone knew everyone else, saw whose chimney was sending out a swirl of smoke, knew who had cause for celebration and who was in need of help. Certainly people quarreled and disagreed, but for the most part they joined together to help each other. They shared big jobs like barn raisings and corn shuckings and entertained themselves with singing schools, writing schools, and berry pickings. Children gathered in the morning as they walked to school, and neighbors communed with one another at church or on mill day. Stories and music upheld their history and helped this community endure for more than a century.

Until the 1920s and 1930s that is, when a whirlwind blew into the Great Smoky Mountains in the form of a new national park.

A "Mountain Culture" Museum

The idea of a national park in the southern Appalachians had been brewing for at least a couple of decades. Spurred by eager local boosterism and surveys by government officials, Congress in 1926 passed and President Calvin Coolidge signed the law that authorized the Secretary of Interior to determine boundaries and accept land and money for a Great Smoky Mountains National Park.

But the Great Smokies was a park in name only, because it literally had to be created out of what was then entirely private land. The states of North Carolina and Tennessee had to raise funds to buy those lands, which they would then donate to the federal government. It took another decade before the complicated process of obtaining more than a half million acres was accomplished.

As the park's boundaries were drawn and redrawn, Cades Cove soon fell within the line. Park organizers recognized that this deep-rooted community likely would resist eviction. High government leaders emphatically assured them that eminent domain—condemnation—would not be employed. In a Knoxville newspaper article headlined "Erroneous Impression Among Mountain Folk That Lands Will Be Condemned," Colonel David Chapman, a leading park advocate, repeated that "It is unfortunate that this idea should have in any way gotten abroad, as there certainly is no grounds for such fear and no authority for anyone to express the probabilities that they should be compelled to relinquish or to be removed from their property at any time except upon their own free will and accord."

Those promises soon proved false. Some saw the handwriting on the wall and sold willingly. By the end of 1933 nearly three-fourths of all Cove farms had been purchased, and the last holdouts were ordered to vacate by January 1, 1936. Among them was John W. Oliver, who faced condemnation proceedings against his 337 acres. In a rancorous and prolonged fight, he took his case all the way to the Tennessee Supreme Court, but he lost. John W. Oliver and his family finally moved out of their beloved Cove in 1937.

A dozen Cove families received lifetime leases and were paid to stay on their land, but the valued community they had known survived only in their memories.

41

With the coming of the national park, several ideas surfaced on how to develop the Cove. Most astounding was a proposal to dam Abrams Creek and flood the Cove with "a pleasure lake for boating and fishing," as one proponent described. The Great Smoky Mountains Conservation Association approved a resolution supporting the lake and sent it to President Franklin D. Roosevelt and the Tennessee Valley Authority. Various government officials vacillated, but by 1934 sentiment had turned against the plan.

FDR's "Tree Army," the Civilian Conservation Corps, soon showed up in the Cove. Company 5427 had their camp by the Missionary Baptist Church, their company numbers spelled out by a carefully planted arrangement of daffodils. The young men built and reconstructed roads, trails, and buildings in the Cove,

With residents going or gone, the National Park Service confronted the challenge of preserving the history of Cades Cove without the farmers and millers and choir singers to bring it alive.

*"What is there to be seen, or what is
there to dream about, in an empty
old barn or an unused mill..."*
—HANS HUTH, 1934

42

The geological story of the Great Smoky Mountains is more visible in Cades Cove than most other places in the national park. The mountains are a result of a collision of continents that began some 300 million years ago.

An Open Window

At the entrance to Cades Cove, the sun sinks behind the mountains and washes the sky in soft pink. A trio of horses nibbles peacefully out in a grassy pasture—one black, one white, one brown. In the settling stillness of dusk, the scene is a timeless one that makes a person feel that Cades Cove and these old Smoky Mountains are the rock of ages.

It's an understandable response to such a beautiful landscape. But only change is certain. Nowhere is that truer than in the history of the earth. That history is told in the language of rocks, the language that explains how the Great Smoky Mountains were made and how this place called Cades Cove came to be.

People who lived in Cades Cove knew about geology, though they may have been interested for different reasons. Of value to them was knowing the location of iron ore for the forge, finding a good chunk of whetstone to sharpen an ax, or bringing in the best rock for millstones to grind their corn. Mountain folks distinguished different rocks by basic names—flintrock, mudrock, slaterock.

Geologists name rocks too, and they look at them very closely. They study minute particles, minerals, sand grains, pebbles, and boulders. From that information, they can say what a rock is made of—and how, where, maybe even when—a particular rock was formed. They widen their eyes to look at the grander scale too, at whole mountain ranges formed over hundreds of millions of years. Then they begin to construct a story that extends not in the time frame of human life, but in time so deep and numbers so large that they quickly become abstract.

47

But it's an exciting tale, this story of earth's long and involved history. In Cades Cove, geologists look through a "window" in the mountains. Much like a cove in an ocean bay, Cades Cove is a carved-out cul de sac, a flat-bottomed oval valley of nearly 2,500 acres—about 3 miles across and 8 to 10 miles long. It sits at 1,800 feet in elevation, a bowl rimmed by mountains rising several thousand feet higher. Other such windows exist in the southern Appalachian Mountains, but Cades Cove is one of only two in the national park. Other nearby examples can be seen at Tuckaleechee, Miller, and Wear coves just beyond the park in Tennessee.

Cades Cove's geological story continues every day. The processes that make the rocks and then wear them down are perpetual.

The short story of Cades Cove is that it was created by the erosion of older rock that exposed younger limestone beneath. But older rocks on top of younger? Isn't that in violation of geologic rules and common sense? To get to the bottom on that, we owe a great deal to more than a century of careful sleuthing by geologists. It should help to set out the complex plot of the longer story of Smoky Mountain geology.

First we make rocks, then we make mountains, then we try our best to tear down the mountains. In the venerable Great Smokies the foundation, the basement, began as sedimentary and igneous rock more than a billion years old, rock that was pressure-cooked into metamorphic gneisses and schists that for the most part are hidden from view in the park.

Along came another lengthy period—about 900 to 700 million years ago—when clays, silts, and sands accumulated in a watery basin and were cemented into a nine-mile-thick stack of rock. This massive collection, known as the Ocoee Supergroup, is seen almost everywhere in the park as dark gray to reddish-brown outcrops along road cuts and other places not obscured by verdant plant life. The Ocoee rocks make up the bulk of the mountains that flank the Cove—Thunderhead Mountain, Rich Mountain, Blanket Mountain, Squires Mountain, and others. The Ocoee Supergroup members started as sedimentary rock but were also cooked and altered, though not to as high a degree as the basement rocks. So they're often referred to as "meta-sedimentary."

About 540 to 450 million years ago, more sediments accumulated on the floor of an ocean. The seabed became the repository for animals and limy precipitates that eventually solidified into limestone. This is the rock that underlies Cades Cove.

This limestone contains fossils, about the only rock in the Smokies that does. Though fairly rare, traces of trilobites, brachiopods, gastropods, and cephalopods speak of the limestone's marine origins. More important are fossilized teeth of a creature called a conodont. Geologists consider conodonts "index" fossils of the era, and get excited about them because conodont color variation gives clues to the presence of oil and gas deposits.

Now with all the rock made, we're ready to manufacture mountains. In fact, probably four significant mountain-building episodes have occurred to create the great Appalachian chain that extends for more than 1,800 miles from Canada to Alabama. But it was the last episode, set into motion about 300 million years ago, that made the Great Smokies. It must have been quite the spectacle, as ancestral Africa collided with North America in what is called the Alleghanian "orogeny," forming the southern Appalachians, the highest mountains in the East. The explanation is part of the grand unifying theory of geology known as plate tectonics, in which whole slabs of continent and ocean crust do-si-do around earth's surface in a global contra dance. Tectonics, writes one geologist, are simply the processes that "crimp and crease the earth's crust." Indeed, a fair amount of crimping and creasing did go on in the Smokies.

Accompanying the head-on collision of the two continental plates, a major break called the Great Smoky fault cut through the region. Along this fault, older rock was shoved an astounding 200 miles westward, catapulting the older layers solidly on top of those younger limestones. Also during this wholesale upheaval, the entire area was squeezed, or compressed, into an archlike structure. Fractures in this arch were weak places where water gained entry, stripping away the overlying rocks until,

voilà, the "window" of Cades Cove was opened.

The continents then parted company, drifted slowly to their present positions, and the Atlantic Ocean intervened. Thus, the crests of the Great Smoky Mountains rose to touch the clouds and snag the mist. But, it is a given that high places erode. For a very long time—the last 200 million years or so—water, ice, and wind, the main agents of erosion, have come calling in the Smokies. Today some thirty tributary streams flow into Cades Cove, all joining the mother stream, Abrams Creek, which enters the top end of the Cove and exits at the bottom by Cable Mill.

The Cove's limestone is especially susceptible to chemical erosion as well, a process that happens fairly rapidly. As the limestone dissolves, the result is sinkholes, ponds, bogs, and caves that serve as unique habitats harboring interesting biological inhabitants and helpful information about past environments. The bedrock limestone is exposed in a few good places along the Cove Loop Road, but it's mostly covered now by a skin of good, moisture-retaining soil brought down from the mountains and spread out in floods.

This geologic story has no end. All the processes that created the rocks and the mountains and that wear them away continue today, here and all over the earth. Abrams Creek, weaving through the heart of Cades Cove, carries the mountains to the sea and the whole cycle starts again.

A Place to Roam ...

Four deer graze peacefully out in the field, heads down, seemingly oblivious to the stream of passing cars and people stopping to watch. Yet at the sound of a snapped twig, the deer raise their heads, their ears go up, and their round dark eyes scan the surroundings for possible danger. Nothing seems more imminent than a woodpecker landing in a tree, and so they turn back to their feeding.

The Virginia whitetail deer, *Odocoileus virginianus*, is incredibly abundant in Cades Cove, and over much of North America for that matter. Everywhere, the species seems to have responded favorably to the ax and the plow, spreading its range to the mountain West to mingle with the western mule deer.

Whitetails in Cades Cove and throughout the Southeast are a smaller version of their northern brethren. A five-year-old buck may stand about three feet high at the shoulder, maybe 150 pounds, while the does weigh less than 130 pounds. The white throat patch, white belly, and long brown tail with white underside make them distinctive. The tail especially—raised like a flag when they turn and dash away—is this animal's signature. In summer, their coat is lighter in weight and reddish in color, turning to gray in winter when they camouflage against leafless trees and gray skies.

Deer possess an exceptional sense of hearing. Smell too is of immense importance to them—an "alarm" scent issues from a gland on their hind legs and is carried on the wind to alert other deer. They are fleet of foot, galloping or running up to thirty-five miles an hour; among hooved animals, only pronghorn are

faster. Whitetails leap fences and change direction on a whim, and they will hide to avoid detection. Photographer Erwin Bauer finds that this animal's outstanding characteristic "is its ability to move quietly, ghostlike over its territory and to practically dissolve into its environment."

Through the year, deer follow a cycle that satisfies their fundamental needs—feeding, procreating, and staying alive for another year. In fall and early winter, usually mid November through early January, the bucks of Cades Cove are focused on attracting a female and fighting off competition. The annual rut is triggered by shorter days and hormonal changes. During the rut a buck's neck swells, and he rubs trees and paws the ground to lure a receptive doe. Bucks also engage in frenzied head bashings and antler lockings with rival males; the victor then follows an individual doe, seeking acceptance if she is ready to breed. All this activity is a big energy drain on the buck. He loses weight and strength, and when finally he loses his antlers it's over until the following spring, when he regrows another set.

About seven months after breeding, fawns are born. In the Cove, the birth season begins in late May and reaches a peak from June 1 until mid July. The does form social groups, and each mom stays close by, nursing her fawn on nutritious rich milk. The spotted youngster, well concealed in the

Open fields bathed in sunshine and ripe with grasses and forbs offer near ideal habitat for white-tailed deer.

Visits to Cades Cove are often rated by the number of deer sighted or the number of bucks in the fields.

grasses, stays put while mom leaves to find food. In only a few weeks the fawn is weaned and is able to follow its mother.

When it comes to food, Cades Cove deer enjoy the best of both worlds. They have grass to graze in the fields, browse plants at the edge of the forest, and acorns in the woods in the fall. Shrubs like hearts-a'-bustin' and sawbrier, along with sourwood saplings, are among their favorite browse, though they'll also dine on all kinds of other sprouts, seedlings, and vines—greenbrier, dogwood, maple, blackgum, white oak, and sassafras. In spring, the deer diet shifts from woody plants to herbs, especially lilies and orchids, "ice cream" plants to them. High in calories and nutrition, these plants are just what females need for giving birth and producing milk for their fawns, and what bucks require

for antler development. Deer are ruminants, with a four-chambered stomach that allows them to eat a lot of food in a hurry, then retreat to a safe place to digest it.

Whitetails were stocked in the southern Appalachian Mountains in the early twentieth century, and in Great Smokies their population exploded in the absence of predators and hunting. In Cades Cove in particular, with a change to a mosaic of forest and open fields, they did very well, until 1971. In that year the Cove deer herd experienced a major die off due to epizootic hemorrhagic disease, or EHD. University of Tennessee biologist Michael Pelton and students started working in the Cove that year and witnessed the before and after. The disease so weakened the deer, said Pelton, that visitors were walking up and petting them. What Pelton and his students then observed was a sudden, "tremendous die off." But, in a year or two, the population had recovered, possibly from other deer coming in from the mountains and from the increased food supply and increased reproduction among those deer that survived. By the late 1970s the Cades Cove deer herd had rebounded to more than 500 animals, a density high by any standards.

Deer numbers stayed high through the late 1970s and 1980s, but park biologists believe there are fewer deer now. They count the deer in the Cove in February, when the animals are frequently out in the fields, to get an estimate on total herd size. They also monitor the deer for disease and parasites. Every other summer a herd "health check" is performed, in which a few deer are examined for parasites. A lower parasite "load" in the Cove deer in recent years suggests a healthier herd, and so far a serious malady seen in western deer, called chronic wasting disease, hasn't shown up in the Cove whitetails.

The big diesel truck turns onto Hyatt Lane and the driver stops the engine. In the long, open bed in the back fifty passengers huddle shoulder to shoulder, bundled in stocking caps, coats, and blankets on piles of warm hay. On the clear October night, the sky over Cades Cove is black satin. Two opposing bright beacons shine, Mars in the east and Venus in the west. Then, the park ranger asks everyone to howl like a coyote. The darkness apparently dismisses inhibitions, and the hayriders fill the silence of the Cove with their howls. Convincing they are, but the "songdogs" apparently aren't fooled. None reply that night.

Yet coyotes certainly live in Cades Cove. They're relative newcomers to the mammal community, with biologists first hearing their lively yips and yelps in the Cove in the mid 1980s. These wily western canines started edging eastward in the early twentieth century, some by a natural expansion of their range, some by introduction. Now they're seen everywhere from the Great Smokies to Central Park in New York.

Canis latrans, the coyote, mostly is a loner and a wide traveler. It moves through the tall grasses of the Cove, keeping close watch and safe distance. Coyotes keep in touch with one another through a riotous repertoire of sounds, and females and males work in tandem to feed

Coyotes, foxes, and bobcats, all predators, often competitors, are thriving in this fertile environment.

a den full of hungry pups. Weighing in at only thirty to forty pounds, coyotes are similar in size to a small German shepherd. Long legs, sizable ears, tawny coat, and their habit of holding their bushy tail down helps distinguish them from domestic dogs.

In Great Smoky Mountains National Park, coyotes roam free. They stalk and pounce on mice in the meadow and eat almost anything else they can find—from insects and berries to woodchucks and deer. Unfortunately, they too readily accept handouts from visitors. To short-circuit that propensity—especially among juvenile coyotes moving about in the fall—park biologists have had to use aversive conditioning techniques, such as beanbags and rubber buckshot to discourage "pan-handling" coyotes.

Eminently adaptable, coyotes may be filling a niche left open by predators like wolves and mountain lions. Early bounty hunters could earn six dollars for a wolf pelt, and wolves soon were eliminated from the Southern mountains. Interestingly, Cades Cove was selected as the best place in the park to reintroduce the red wolf in the 1990s. But the experiment didn't take—a virus afflicted the animals, the pups died, there wasn't enough small prey, and the wolves interbred with coyotes.

Mountain lions—or "painters" as they're known in the mountains—were hunted out too, though occasional sightings are reported to rangers each year. Still, no evidence has been received to confirm their presence, and sightings may actually be of captive mountain lions irresponsibly released by their owners.

Mountain lions and wolves were top predators in the past in the Cove. Now it's coyotes, bobcats, and black bears. The predator-prey relationship is complicated by competition between bear, deer, and other animals for food, especially for acorns in the fall. And that ties in to the disappearance of the American chestnut.

In 1905, nearly one-third of all the trees in the forest around Cades Cove were chestnuts. By the 1920s an introduced fungus brought a blight that wiped out chestnuts throughout the Appalachians. One of the last stands of the species in the Great Smokies grew on the ridge between Gregory Mountain and Ekaneetlee Gap above the Cove. But by the 1940s, the chestnuts were mostly gone.

Their absence left a gaping hole in the forest ecosystem, not to mention loss of a staple food for bears and other wildlife. Bear hunter and Cove resident Maynard Ledbetter commented that a person "had to go halfway up Smoky Mountain to find a bear. . .back when there were chestnuts, bear got so fat they couldn't run fast."

Yet bears did occasionally appear in the Cove, and residents had to keep close watch on their beehives and fruit orchards. Charlie Myers, the miller at Cable Mill for many years, told of a bear up in one of his apple trees, taking the fruit right off the branches. In defense he tied his dog to the tree to scare away the bear. The dog got loose around "dusky dark" one evening, and Charlie went out to tie him up again. A loud crack sent the dog running toward Charlie, knocking him down. Looking up, Charlie saw the reason why. The bear was up the tree and, as Charlie related, "He pulled off a limb big as my arm, full of apples. The apples rained down on me." The

bear was so close Charlie could hear his teeth popping. "I could have reached up and touched him and he could have reached down and snapped my head."

But with protection in the national park, and the maturing forest, black bears found a sanctuary and their population began to rebound. Estimates were up to 600, then 800, then as high as 2,000 bears in the 1990s. By 2005, some 1,400 bears were believed to be living in the 800 square miles of the Smokies, one of the highest population densities of black bear in the East.

Today the Cades Cove bear population is governed by the amount of "mast," both hard and soft—acorns, hickory nuts, beech nuts, berries, wild grapes, and black cherries. There are good mast years and bad mast years, determined by weather and climate fluctuations.

Unlike chestnuts, which produced reliably every year, oaks yield a good crop of acorns only about one in five years. When mast is scarce, female bears are poorly nourished and experience low or almost no reproduction. The reverse occurs in good mast years.

Around late April or early May, as the grass greens up and bloodroot and trillium bloom, a black bear cub enters a brave new world in Cades Cove when it emerges from the den with mom. The cub, and maybe a sibling, was born in the den in January or February; by the time it ventures forth it weighs about five pounds. Mom remains weak from giving birth, nursing, and remaining inactive for three or four months. She and her youngsters are famished when they come out, and they comb the woods for something to eat. A succulent plant called squawroot is available, along with a few fresh sprigs of new growth.

The bears draw on their fat deposits and will even lose weight until berries are ripe in June and July. The cub eats and grows through the summer, gaining another thirty pounds, learning to scamper up trees, tumbling with a brother or sister, and generally enjoying a footloose and fancy-free life, under mom's close eye. Between feedings, the young bear rests in the shade in a summer bed.

Summer is also the season of breeding for bears. Males fight over females and sear tree trunks with bites and scratches. After breeding, the egg does not implant in the female bear's uterus until late fall. Delayed implantation means she doesn't have to be pregnant while she's trying to feed through the summer, and it's a fallback strategy for those years when food stocks are inadequate. If the mast crop fails, the

egg will be reabsorbed, no cubs are born, and the female has a better chance of surviving the winter and reproducing the following year.

At the end of summer and into early autumn, both female and male bears must pack on pounds before entering dens for another winter. Bears may be oblivious to the gorgeous fall colors in the Cove, but they're not unaware of the supply of acorns. Autumn is the time of the "fall shuffle." Bears climb oak trees for first dibs on acorns and consume the crop of black cherries in the Cove. A bear can gain 20 to 40 percent of its body weight, most of it as fat, in only a few weeks during this feeding frenzy. This is when bears, especially yearling males, are moving beyond the summer range and become more vulnerable to accidents or poachers.

Many families in the mountains kept bees. Defending their hives from bears was a frequent struggle for which the shotgun was generally the tool of choice.

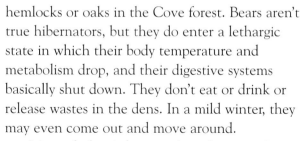

hemlocks or oaks in the Cove forest. Bears aren't true hibernators, but they do enter a lethargic state in which their body temperature and metabolism drop, and their digestive systems basically shut down. They don't eat or drink or release wastes in the dens. In a mild winter, they may even come out and move around.

Most of what is known about bears in the Great Smokies and Cades Cove—their numbers, movements, and behavior—comes from a long-term study started by Michael Pelton and his students in 1969. For close to forty years researchers have hiked to trap sites, climbed trees, crawled through laurel thickets, even entered dens to capture, collar, mark, measure, probe, and recapture bears. They also obtain hair samples to do DNA analysis and identify individual animals, making the park's bears among the best studied in the country.

Information from that work also helps with a major problem in the Cove—some call it bear management, others call it people management. Mainly, it involves keeping bears and people apart, to protect both parties. The sight of a single bear is a sure-fire way to cause a major traffic snarl along the Cades Cove Loop Road, and some visitors can't resist trying to get closer for a better picture. Bears also visit Cades Cove Picnic Area on occasion, especially at night, investigating dumpsters or any other garbage or food that might be available. Once a bear becomes accustomed to human food— "food conditioned" as biologists say—it will do everything in its power to get that food, even breaking windows in vehicles to reach a cooler.

From mid November to mid January, depending on weather and the mast supply, bears enter winter dens. Prime den sites, especially for females, are cavities up in 200-year-old eastern

Historically, a large number of bears that have had to be captured and relocated in the park have been from Cades Cove.

Every person—camper, hiker, sightseer—needs to practice vigilance to assure that the bears of Cades Cove and the Smokies remain healthy and wild. No matter how warm and fuzzy bears look, they are not stuffed toys and this is not a zoo. These amazing animals—with their memories, dexterity, agility, and tolerance—are still wild. They are top-of-the-food-chain creatures, and we are their only predators. Black bears will do just fine in Cades Cove, if only they are left to do what they do best.

Bear 287

*I*f you think your life is stressful, here's a story that may lend some perspective. It's about a black bear in the Great Smokies known as Number 287.

Her saga began in 1997, when she was captured and released over the Fourth of July weekend in the Cades Cove Picnic Area. A few weeks later, Bear 287 returned and crawled inside a dumpster foraging for food. Along came the garbage truck, making its rounds, emptying that dumpster, and compacting the trash as it went—all the time with the unknown passenger inside. That afternoon the bear was discovered when the truck disgorged its load at the county waste facility. The traumatized creature literally climbed the walls and was hanging from the rafters when a wildlife officer tranquilized her. A bucket truck got her down, and she was off to the University of Tennessee Veterinary College for observation. The bear didn't look good. She was understandably slow and lethargic and had suffered serious bruising and damage to her urinary tract.

But miraculously, Bear 287 improved and finally recovered well enough to be released again back in the park, but in a location forty miles from Cades Cove.

Seven years later, in May 2004, she was back in the Cove picnic area. Despite attempts to keep her away, the brazen bruin continued to prowl the grounds and enter another dumpster. Once again it was recapture, treat for teeth problems, then relocate to a spot sixty miles away in the Cherokee National Forest.

In August 2005, she was back again, this time with a male cub in tow. Both were escorted to the national forest. By this time Bear 287's fame had spread. She was cast as a fictitious character in a children's book, The Troublesome Cub, *but in truth she's no cub. At age sixteen, she's four times as old as the average female bear in the park.*

Meanwhile, back in Cades Cove everyone is waiting and watching, and nobody is placing bets on whether this mighty determined bear will make yet another appearance.

Restored grasslands in the Cove offer both food and shelter for wildlife. Native meadow plants like big and little bluestem, Indian grass, blazing star, and sunflowers are being propagated or protected by the park's resource management staff.

... And A Place To Hide

For its size, the floor of Cades Cove probably holds more species diversity than any other place in the park because so many special habitats exist—roadsides, meadows, limestone sinkholes and wetlands, caves, canebrakes, large springs, and the creekside forest. This means lots of places for small mammals, birds, reptiles, amphibians, and fish to live. These smaller but no less important creatures in sheer mass account for the greatest share of the wildlife biomass in the Cove. For visitors, they provide endless hours of delightful observation.

Visible along the loop road, especially in springtime, are rotund rodents in grizzled yellow-brown. They're woodchucks, better known to some as groundhogs, the forecasters of spring in the East. They perch atop the mounded rim of a burrow opening, looking for fresh green grass in the spring, ears perked, ever alert to the presence of a fox or hawk. Woodchucks do best when they can stay in touch with other woodchucks, touching noses and keeping eye contact with each other, endlessly enchanting to any humans lucky enough to observe them.

In the Cove, they reach the farthest southern part of their range. Originally forest dwellers, woodchucks had little trouble adapting to open fields and woods, finding plenty of food along fence rows and in old orchards. The Cove's loamy soils make for good burrowing. Mostly solitary, only a single woodchuck inhabits a tidy, grass-lined underground tunnel system. It may also dig "auxiliary" burrows for refuge while eating or moving about. In winter, woodchucks hibernate in dens in wooded or brushy places, and in summer they move to

open flats or rolling land. Like bears, woodchucks spend a good part of the summer building up fat reserves to carry them through winter hibernation, then lose all that weight over the next six months.

Woodchuck burrows cohouse several other small mammals in Cades Cove, including foxes, cottontails, skunks, and raccoons. Raccoons—unmistakable in their black face "masks" and ringed tails—are related to bears and dogs. They are out mainly at night dipping into streams and ponds for

Woodchuck, red fox, cottontail rabbit, and many other mammals thrive in the verdant meadows of Cades Cove. Acre for acre, the Cove shelters a larger population of creatures great and small than nearly any other area of the park.

A river runs through it. Abrams Creek is home to rainbow trout, salamanders, shiners, chubs, crayfish, and their many predators.

frogs and crayfish, or prowling for young turtles or birds. These carnivores are admirably dexterous in manipulating food with their front paws. In the daytime raccoons usually bed down, often in the burrow of a woodchuck. Though such burrows are plentiful in the Cove, if already occupied there may be some competition. Raccoons also use rock crevices, barns, and trees, especially red oaks, as day beds. The site they choose depends on the season and

when they are about to give birth. In one study in the Cove, female raccoons preferred tree dens as maternity sites, the leafy nests cooler in summer and freer of insects.

Breeding among Cove raccoons peaks in April. The pregnant female enters a den and gives birth in June, usually to three or four young. They all stay together in the den for about two months. Even after they come out, mom invests lots of energy into taking care of her young and watching as the little ones circle up a tree trunk to hide. Raccoons live about four years, and one in the Cove lived to the ripe old age of seven. By that time, poor physical condition makes them prime prey for foxes, bobcats, owls, and wild dogs.

63

Limestone often gives rise to caves, and caves shelter bats. This is true in Cades Cove and nearby, with eight or so different species netted in recent years. Among them is the endangered Indiana bat. This small gray-brown myotis forms large hibernating colonies in winter, and one of the largest in the region—several thousand bats—occupies a large cave not far from Cades Cove. The Cove produced a big first with the discovery of female Indiana bats, both pregnant and lactating, the first records of reproductive females from the southern Appalachians. Previously it was thought that all female Indiana bats migrated north during the summer breeding season. Still, overall the Indiana bat has seen a precipitous drop in numbers throughout its eastern range; the reasons are not clear, but loss of preferred old trees and use of pesticides are suspected. If more

Every season unfolds with new life. Wildflowers erupt in April, reach a crescendo in summer, and continue strong into late autumn.

Birdwatchers flock to the Cove to see water-fowl, warblers, birds of prey, and enormous Wild Turkey.

Two factors add to the abundance of life: limestone and sunlight. Cades Cove soil is less acidic than much of the Smokies and more sunlight reaches the ground.

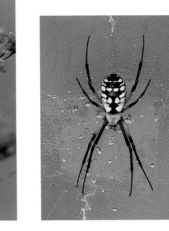

In Cades Cove resides the increasingly rare opportunity to preserve a whole, intact, ecosystem, a whole web of life, for the benefit of future generations.

reproducing females and maternity colonies are found, there is greater hope for the species' survival.

Cades Cove is a good place to see a different cast of birds too. A chorus of Wild Turkey calls fills the fog-bound meadows in early morning. Wild Turkey have done well here among fields and forest edge, feeding in flocks on plentiful beech nuts, acorns, and blackgum fruits. In springtime the Toms gobble, strut, and fan their tails, showing off for the ladies. Birdwatchers will also be rewarded with observations of water-fowl not found elsewhere in the park—Wood Ducks, Green Herons, and Yellow-crowned Night-herons for example. As one of the few grassy areas in the park, the Cove is the place to see grassland birds— Eastern Meadowlarks warbling from fenceposts, Northern Bobwhite quail whistling their name-sake call, and vultures and hawks soaring over-head. In the west end, trees along an oxbow of Abrams Creek have offered exciting sightings of majestic Golden Eagles.

Another symphony tunes up in the Cove on wet spring evenings with the sharp bleeps of Spring Peepers and the rasps of Chorus Frogs. They belong to the amphibian clan—frogs, toads, and salamanders—a group so numerous in the Great Smoky Mountains and Cades Cove that scientists come from all over to study them.

Most amphibians are tied to water for at least part of their lives, and water is an element of phenomenal abundance in the Great Smokies. The Cove itself receives more than fifty

inches of rain a year, on average. Abrams Creek, the Cove's main waterway, may have served as a wet corridor from the Tennessee Valley into the drier pine-oak of western Cades Cove, enriching amphibian life here, especially among the frogs. Abrams Creek is also the only place in the park to find mudpuppies and map turtles.

But Cades Cove also holds standing water, a definite rarity in the park. Bogs, marshes, swamps, sinkhole ponds, and other wetlands host a slew of salamanders and frogs. Two rare species—the Mole Salamander and Eastern Spadefoot—can be found in Gum Swamp on the south side of Cades Cove. The Mole Salamander and four others depend on ponds and standing water for breeding, while Cave and Long-tailed salamanders are even more exacting in their requirements—they develop in pools only inside caves found in the Cove. Amphibians are the focus of much attention because some species have exhibited body malformations and disturbing declines in numbers. The question is whether these are warning signs of wider environmental deterioration such as acid precipitation, or whether they are part of the normal ebb and flow of the complex, highly variable lives of these animals. Long-term monitoring is the best way to get at the answer, and Cades Cove amphibians are key subjects in that effort.

Fisheries biologists have been keeping track of a rare fish called the Flame chub that lives in springs associated with Abrams Creek. It's a small population, the only one known in the Little Tennessee River system, rendering this chub a species of special concern. The name comes from the striking orange color of the males at breeding time—park biologist Steve Moore calls them "footballs with fins on." A diverse lot of other native fish occurs in Abrams Creek, including darters, hogsuckers, and Tennessee and Warpaint shiners. The limestone-based water gives rise to a healthy supply of insects, food upon which rainbow trout also

thrive. The nonnative rainbows were stocked in Abrams and other park streams in the early twentieth century, and now a reproducing wild population is doing quite well. Native brook trout, however, did not survive the warming and sedimentation caused by intensive agriculture and large-scale logging.

Cades Cove's other specialties are on display in the plant world. The meadows are swatches of prairie, with short and tall grasses such as bluestems and Indian grass. Signature of the Cove, Indian grass greens up and matures in the summer months. In early fall the ripe seed heads form silky plumes of gold, earning it another common name, "goldstem." The nutritious seeds are gobbled up by Bobwhite Quail, Bobolinks, and meadowlarks, and the six-foot-tall stems provide fine cover for animals. The native grasses tend to grow in clumps, leaving paths open where animals can travel and forage. The Cove's "midwestern" feel is displayed by the presence of other plants that reach their farthest eastern limits here—ones

Old Remedies, New Prescriptions

*I*n caring for Cades Cove, the Park Service strives to do two things—maintain the historic openness and views and encourage natural processes—both at the same time. It's a fine line to walk at times.

Once Great Smoky Mountains National Park was established, the forest started growing in on the Cove meadows. First, understory plants like sourwood and dogwood encroached, followed by larger trees like eastern hemlocks and white pines. To keep the meadows open, fields were leased for haying and cattle grazing (nearly 1,500 head at one point). Through the years other management

actions were taken—mowing, suppressing fires completely, draining wetlands and channelizing Abrams Creek, and introducing nonnative fescue and lespedeza.

With time, an artificial agricultural scene was created in the Cove. Old photos and the accounts of former residents told of something different. More authentic was a patchwork quilt of small fields, some of them fallow; briarpatches; woodlots; small pastures; and orchards.

By the late 1970s and early 1980s, land management practices were showing effects on the native animals, plants, and aquatic systems of the Cove too. Grazing and fertilizing brought problems of erosion, siltation, and heavy nutrient loads in Abrams Creek; the thick mats of fescue proved bad wildlife habitat; and native species often were outcompeted.

The Park Service decided to take corrective steps, recognizing the irony that once there was a true historic scene, it was mostly obliterated, and now it would be restored. This time, the park would also concentrate on bringing back part of the naturalness of the Cove. To that end, cattle were fenced away from the stream, fences enclosing large fields were removed, and haying and grazing ended in the late 1990s.

A key tool—fire—is now being reintroduced under particular "prescriptions" of temperature, humidity, and winds. Cycled through selected fields over several years, fire may reduce the dominant fescue and encourage taller native bluestems and Indian grass. In addition, several native grasses are being grown for seed in "increase" fields in the Cove, and are replanted in interior fields.

Mowing is still used on interior fields and so-called "viewshed" fields along the loop road so visitors will still see wildlife. The mowing schedule is timed to avoid the peak of deer fawning and to protect small mammals and ground-nesting birds such as Bobwhite Quail.

Wetlands and stream channels are also being restored by rejuvenating the meandering path of Abrams Creek, reinforcing streambanks, plugging drainage ditches, and nurturing ponds and wet *places to encourage willows, wild iris, water striders, wood frogs, and other native inhabitants. A significant and much endangered riparian plant—American river cane—is of concern for its great importance as food and cover for wildlife. Much effort is also being applied to remove exotic species that are especially invasive in the Cove—among animals wild boars wreak havoc in wet areas, and among plants Japanese stilt grass and European orchard grass are tough targets.*

Even native animals can lead to problems if their populations rise too high. Park biologists have been monitoring plants to see how deer browsing has influenced them. Though some wildflowers such as violets and wood sorrel can survive or recover from intense browsing, others don't fare as well. Trilliums are an example. Deer love trilliums in the spring; one chomp and they can take out a large specimen and leave nothing stored in the root to allow the plant to come back another year. Large colonies of trilliums were noted in the woodlots of Cades Cove in the 1940s and 1950s. Now they are rare or not thriving. A ten-year study in the Cove fenced deer out of certain plots; results suggested that heavy browsing does not favor sweet white trillium and Catesby's trillium. A rare orchid and Virginia chain fern are gone, possible casualties of overbrowsing. However, a rare gentian called American columbo was also of concern, but it started to come back with fewer deer in the mid 1990s.

And so for Cades Cove, both old remedies and new prescriptions may combine to keep both human and natural worlds in good health.

like climbing bittersweet, blazing star, Virginia bluebell, and yellow mandarin.

Some of the plants are limestone lovers, which means their habitat is limited in the park. Others are here for unknown reasons, but their very rarity earns the designation of "critically imperiled." Most aren't household names—marsh bellflower, longleaf stitchwort, hairy willow-herb, and yellow-eyed grass—but that only adds to their fascination. Certain oaks—scarlet, blackjack, and post oaks—are more likely found in the drier pine-oak forests in the west end of the Cove as well. Then there's the sweetgum, buttonwood, and quillwort growing in the wet Gum Swamp near the Cable Cemetery, far from their home range on the Atlantic coast; botanists don't really have a good explanation for their presence here. More in place, but still rare, are traditional woodland flowers like Catesby's trillium and a few orchids found in moist, shaded nooks along the Rich Mountain and Cooper roads leading out of the Cove.

Protecting and perpetuating Cades Cove's special naturalness is an ongoing job. Another large challenge is dealing with the sheer number of visitors. Some two million people come each year, giving the Cove the dubious distinction of being one of the most visited places in the most visited national park in the country. People wind slowly around the narrow, eleven-mile, one-way loop road in their vehicles. They stop for a closer look at a deer or a bear, and pull off to walk up to an old cabin, church, or cemetery. Such a concentration of humanity and cars in a relatively small area means significant management and environmental problems, problems the park and the public are studying and hoping to solve.

"an exquisite creation ... [that] has a strong hold on all those who have known its solitudes and its glories."
—WILLIAM O. DOUGLAS, 1962